Pennie Stoyles and Peter Pentland

The A to Z of
Inventions
and Inventors

Volume 5: Q to S

Smart Apple Media

This edition first published in 2006 in the United States of America by Smart Apple Media.
Reprinted 2007 (twice)

Smart Apple Media
2140 Howard Drive West
North Mankato
Minnesota 56003

First published in 2006 by
MACMILLAN EDUCATION AUSTRALIA PTY LTD
15-19 Claremont Street, South Yarra, Australia 3141

Visit our website at www.macmillan.com.au

Associated companies and representatives throughout the world.

Copyright © Pennie Stoyles and Peter Pentland 2006

Library of Congress Cataloging-in-Publication Data

Stoyles, Pennie.
    The A to Z of inventions and inventors / Pennie Stoyles and Peter Pentland.
    p. cm.
    Contents: v. 1 A to B – v. 2. C to F – v. 3. G to L – v. 4. M to P – v. 5. Q-S – v.6 T-Z.
    ISBN-13: 978-1-58340-804-9 (v. 1)
    ISBN-13: 978-1-58340-805-6 (v. 2)
    ISBN-13: 978-1-58340-788-2 (v. 3)
    ISBN-13: 978-1-58340-789-9 (v. 4)
    ISBN-13: 978-1-58340-790-5 (v. 5)
    ISBN-13: 978-1-58340-791-2 (v. 6)
    1. Inventions—History—20th century—Encyclopedias. 2. Inventors—Biography—Encyclopedias.
    I. Pentland, Peter. II. Title.
    T20.S76 2006
    608.03—dc22   2005057602

Edited by Sam Munday
Text and cover design by Ivan Finnegan, iF design
Page layout by Ivan Finnegan, iF design
Photo research by Legend Images
Illustrations by Alan Laver, Shelly Communications

Printed in USA

Acknowledgments
The author and the publisher are grateful to the following for permission to reproduce copyright material:

Front cover: photo of skateboard courtesy of Photodisc

Photos courtesy of:
The Advertising Archives, p. 25; Coo-ee Picture Library, p. 26; Early Office Museum (www.earlyofficemuseum.com), p. 28; Getty Images, p. 22; Legendimages, pp. 12, 31; NEC, p. 10; Photolibrary, p. 6 (top); Photolibrary/Index Stock Imagery, p. 15; Photolibrary/Leanne Temme, p. 30; Photolibrary/Library of Congress/Science Photo Library, p. 8; Photolibrary/Susumu Nishinaga/Science Photo Library, p. 9; Photolibrary/Workbook, Inc., p. 4; Photoobjects, © 2005 JupiterImages Corporation, pp. 6 (bottom), 14, 24; Photos.com, p. 18; Rob Cruse Photography, pp. 16, 20, 21, 27; Bill Thomas/ Imagen, p. 19.

While every care has been taken to trace and acknowledge copyright, the publisher tenders their apologies for any accidental infringement where copyright has proved untraceable. Where the attempt has been unsuccessful, the publisher welcomes information that would redress the situation.

Inventions

Welcome to the exciting world of inventions.

The A to Z of Inventions and Inventors is about inventions that people use every day. Sometimes these inventions happen by accident. Sometimes they come from a moment of inspiration. Often they are developed from previous inventions. In some cases, inventors race against each other to invent a machine.

Volume 5: Q to S inventions

Qwerty keyboard
Radio
Record player
Refrigerator
Roll-on deodorant
Rubber bands
Saccharin
Safety pin
Scrabble®
Skateboard
Sliced bread
Soft drink
Stapler
Sunscreen

They said it!

"The radio craze . . . will die out in time."
Thomas Edison, 1922

Qwerty keyboard

The Qwerty keyboard is the name of the arrangement of letters on a typewriter or a computer keyboard. It is named after the first six keys on the top alphabet row of the keyboard.

Who invented the Qwerty keyboard?

Christopher Sholes invented the first commercial typewriter in the United States in 1872. An important part of the design was the Qwerty keyboard.

The Qwerty keyboard story

Christopher Sholes made the first typewriter to be mass-produced and sold. The first typewriters were mechanical. When the letter key was pressed, an arm would fly up and stamp the letter onto the paper. If you typed very quickly, the arms could jam together and get stuck. The Qwerty keyboard was designed to reduce jams so you could type more quickly.

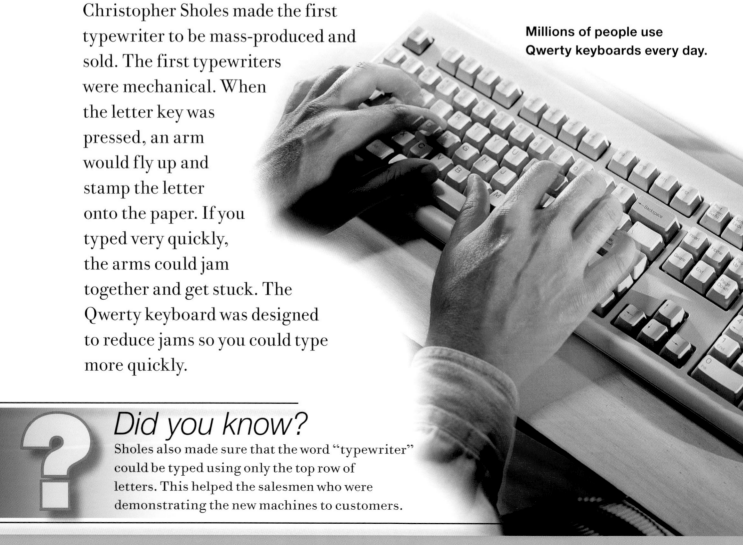

Millions of people use Qwerty keyboards every day.

Did you know?

Sholes also made sure that the word "typewriter" could be typed using only the top row of letters. This helped the salesmen who were demonstrating the new machines to customers.

How Qwerty keyboards work

When designing his keyboard, Sholes studied letters that were often typed one after the other, like "s" and "h". He made sure that the keys for the common pairs of letters were far apart so that they would not jam.

Qwerty keyboard

Dvorak keyboard

Changes to Qwerty keyboards over time

In 1932, August Dvorak designed a new keyboard that he thought was more "user-friendly." He put letters that were often typed together next to each other. Nobody wanted to learn how to type on a different keyboard, so it was not a success. It seems that the Qwerty keyboard is here to stay.

Related invention

The idea of a typewriter was **patented** by Henry Mill, an English engineer, in 1714. It wasn't until 1808 that the first working typewriter was made by Pellegrino Turri of Italy.

Glossary word

patented   applying a right granted to make, use, or sell something which is new, inventive, or useful.

5

Radio is a way of sending information such as speech or music through space using electrical waves.

Who invented radio?

Italian scientist, Guglielmo Marconi, invented radio in 1897.

Guglielmo Marconi (1874–1937) invented the radio.

The radio story

Marconi was a scientist who started experimenting with radio waves in 1894. Three years later he sent a message to a tugboat 18 miles (29 km) away. Later he was able to send a morse code message across the Atlantic Ocean.

The first main use of radio was to send messages across water to places that the telegraph system could not reach. The earliest radio **receivers** were linked to telegraph printers.

Radio stations were set up in the 1920s to broadcast programmes that could be received in people's homes.

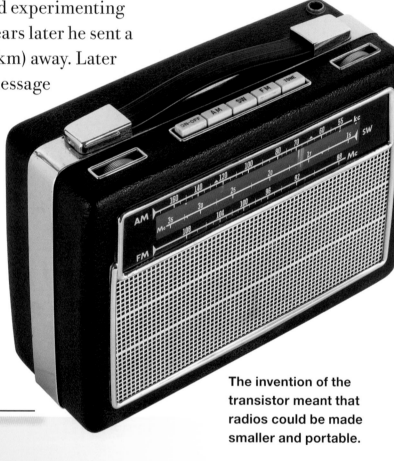

The invention of the transistor meant that radios could be made smaller and portable.

*R*adio timeline

1888	1894	1906	1921
German scientist Heinrich Hertz discovered radio waves	Marconi started to experiment with radio waves	The first broadcasts of speech were made in the U.S. and Germany	The first regular broadcasting stations began operating

How radio works

Radio signals are sent out from a **transmitter**. The transmitter changes speech or music into radio waves and sends them out in all directions.

There are lots of radio stations and transmitters sending signals at the same time. A radio receiver can be tuned to one of the signals at a time. It then processes the radio wave and turns it back into speech or music.

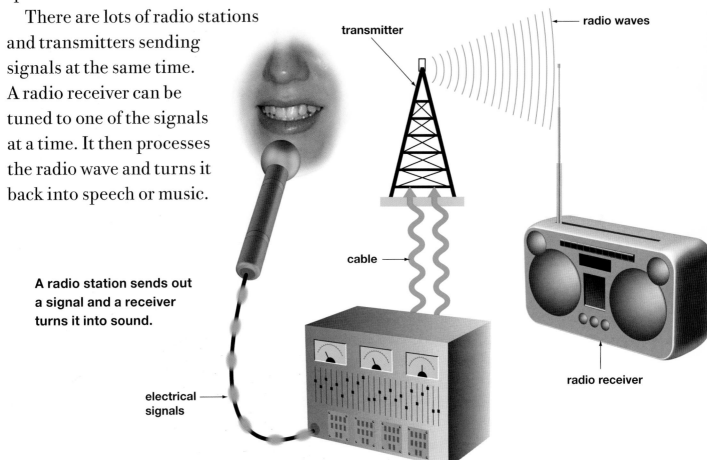

transmitter

radio waves

cable

electrical signals

radio receiver

A radio station sends out a signal and a receiver turns it into sound.

Changes to radio over time

Radio can now transmit music in stereo and even digitally, so that people can listen to a high quality of sound.

Related inventions

American engineer Karl Jansky invented the radio telescope in 1931. It uses a huge dish to receive radio waves from space. The radio waves might be coming from distant space probes, stars, or galaxies.

Glossary words

receivers	devices that detect radio waves and turn them into sound
transmitter	device that sends radio waves

Record player

Record players are part of a family of machines known collectively as phonographs. They reproduce sound using a needle that runs along a groove in a record.

Who invented the record player?

The first type of record player, the phonograph, was invented by the American inventor, Thomas Edison (1847–1931).

The record player story

Thomas Edison was trying to improve the **telegraph** system, which sent messages through wires in Morse code using short bursts of electricity.

He made a machine with a cylinder, a crank handle device, a needle for recording and a separate needle to play back the sound, a mouthpiece, and a listening cone.

In 1877, Edison put tinfoil on the cylinder, cranked the handle and shouted, "Mary had a little lamb" into the mouthpiece. When he played it back he clearly heard the rhyme.

Thomas Edison with his phonograph, which was the first type of record player.

Did you know?

Record players were first used as sideshow novelties. Edison even used them to make the first talking dolls.

How a record player works

A record has a single groove that starts at the outer edge and ends in the center. As the record turns, a needle rides in the groove. The sides of the groove make the needle vibrate and produce electrical signals. The signals are carried by wires to an amplifier and then to a loudspeaker, which makes sound waves in the air.

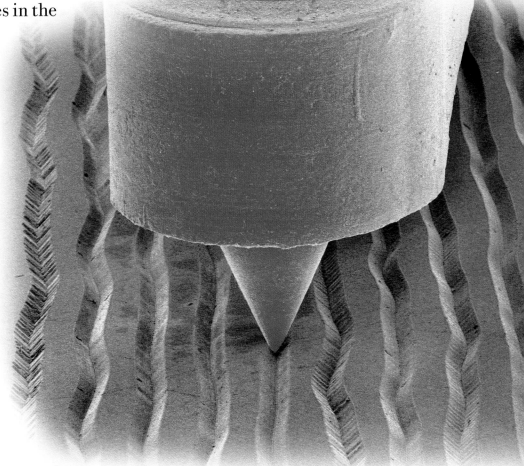

The sides of the groove in a record make the needle vibrate.

Changes to record players over time

Records were replaced by compact discs in the 1990s. By the early 2000s, music was being stored and played back using small portable computers.

Related invention

The tape recorder was invented in 1898. It was built by a Danish inventor called Valdemar Poulsen. It used a steel wire instead of the plastic tape used today.

Glossary word

telegraph   a way to send messages along wires using short bursts of electricity

Refrigerator

A refrigerator is a machine used to produce low temperatures. It is mainly used to keep food cool and fresh.

Who invented the refrigerator?

Karl von Linde, a German, invented the modern refrigerator in 1871.

The refrigerator story

In 1834 an American, Jacob Perkins, became the first person to make a machine that froze water. Karl von Linde made the first modern-style refrigerator in 1871. Gas kept inside a sealed system of pipes was used to carry heat from the inside to the outside of the refrigerator.

In 1873, Scottish-born Australian James Harrison wanted to freeze meat and send it to Europe for sale, so he built a big refrigerator on a ship. Unfortunately no one knew how to work the machine and the first shipment was ruined.

Household refrigerators only became common after the end of World War II.

Refrigerators keep food fresh by keeping it cool.

Did you know?

In 1806 an American, Frederick Tudor, started collecting ice from frozen ponds in Boston and sending it by ship to people who lived in the tropics. Tudor packed the ice in sawdust to keep it cool during its journey.

How refrigerators work

Refrigerators have a closed system of pipes. Gas called a refrigerant is squashed into a liquid by a compressor and flows through a long pipe outside the refrigerator. It loses heat and passes to a wide pipe inside the refrigerator. The liquid changes back into a gas and takes heat from inside the refrigerator, cooling the food. The pipe carries the gas back to the compressor and the process is repeated.

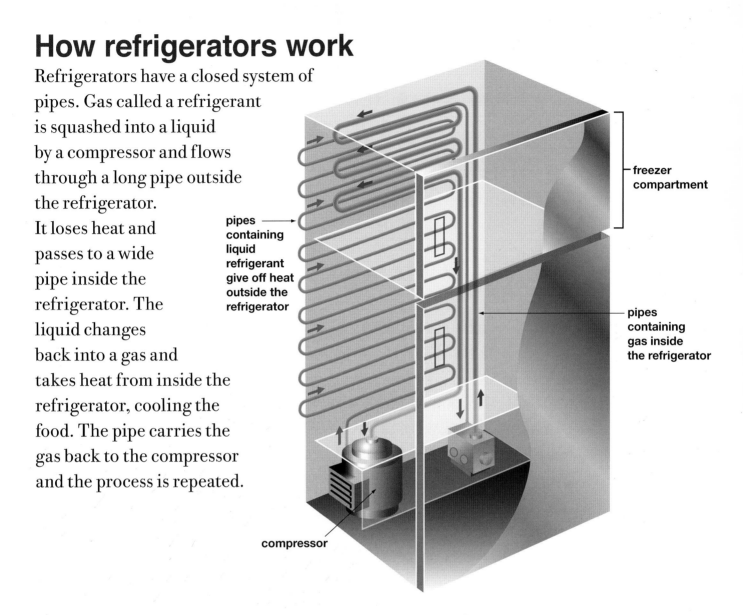

pipes containing liquid refrigerant give off heat outside the refrigerator

freezer compartment

pipes containing gas inside the refrigerator

compressor

Changes to refrigerators over time

Refrigerators once used gases that harmed the environment. These gases would escape when the refrigerators were thrown away. Refrigerators today use environmentally friendly gases.

Related invention

Airconditioners use refrigeration machines to cool air. The modern air conditioner was invented by an American engineer, Willis Carrier, in 1902.

Roll-on deodorant

Deodorant is a substance that stops body odor caused by sweat, usually under your arms. Roll-on deodorant has a special rolling ball which helps spread the deodorant evenly.

Who invented roll-on deodorant?

Roll-on deodorant was invented by Helen Barnett Diserens in 1952 in the U.S.

The roll-on deodorant story

The first deodorants were creams that you put on with your fingers. The cream often left marks on your clothes and you had to wash your hands after using them. Helen Barnett Diserens was a researcher at a company that made cream deodorants. She was inspired by the ballpoint pen, which had recently been discovered. She designed a glass deodorant container based on the same principle. The container is sometimes called a "deroller."

The rolling ball spreads deodorant evenly.

Deodorant timeline

1888	1940s	1952	1965
The first deodorant was sold	Solid stick deodorants were invented	Roll-on deodorant was invented	The first aerosol deodorant was sold

How roll-on deodorant works

The liquid inside the bottle is a lotion containing "active ingredients." When you roll the ball, a thin layer of lotion is transferred from inside the bottle onto your skin. There are two different types of active ingredients in roll-ons. Antiperspirants work by clogging the sweat glands so that they cannot release sweat. Deodorants work by neutralizing the smell of the sweat and by killing the bacteria which produce bad smells.

Sweat is produced by sweat glands in your skin.

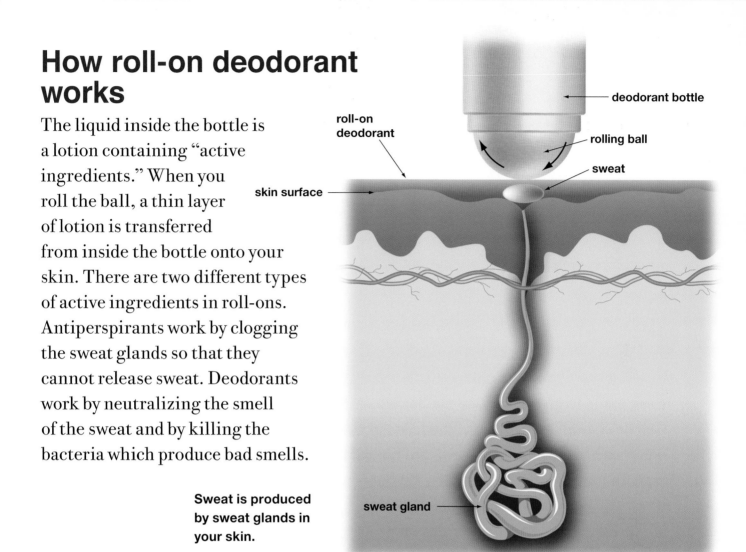

deodorant bottle

roll-on deodorant

rolling ball

sweat

skin surface

sweat gland

Changes to roll-on deodorant over time

The first aerosol antiperspirant was introduced in 1965. Antiperspirants soon became more popular than roll-ons. Not long after, scientists found that the propellants used in aerosol cans harmed the environment. People stopped using so many aerosols and today, roll-on deodorants are more popular than aerosol deodorants.

Related inventions

Hungarian brothers, Laszlo and Georg Biro, invented the first non-leaking ballpoint pen in 1935. The computer mouse was invented using the rolling ball from a roll-on deodorant.

Rubber bands

Rubber bands are stretchy loops of rubber.

Who invented rubber bands?

Rubber bands were invented in 1845 in England by Stephen Perry.

The rubber band story

Stephen Perry was a businessman and inventor who owned a rubber manufacturing company in London, England. He was a tidy man and liked to keep his office papers in neat piles. He invented rubber bands to hold his papers and envelopes together. The rubber bands were made from vulcanized rubber which had been invented by Charles Goodyear in 1839. The first rubber was not very stretchy and would snap if placed in the sun for too long. Vulcanized rubber is natural rubber which has been heated and processed so that it stays stretchy. Stephen Perry patented the rubber band on March 17, 1845.

Rubber bands can be made in all sorts of sizes.

Did you know?

In 1770, Joseph Priestly noticed that balls of latex could rub out pencil marks, so the name "rubber" was invented.

How rubber bands work

Rubber bands stretch because of the shape of the molecules they are made from. Imagine a bowl of cooked spaghetti, where every single strand is linked to each other at certain points. This is what a rubber band would look like under a microscope. You can stretch it and the strands stay linked to each other and spring back. If you stretch it too much, the links between the strands break and so will the rubber band.

Natural rubber is made from latex which comes from the bark of a rubber tree.

Changes to rubber bands over time

In the 1920s and 1930s, the demand for rubber increased due to the use of cars. Rubber was needed for tires. There was not enough natural rubber, so scientists searched for other ways to make rubber. Today, rubber is made from petroleum and coal.

Related invention

In 1871, a Frenchman called Alphonse Penaud invented the first rubber band-powered model airplane. He called it a *planaphore* and it flew 131 feet (40 m).

Saccharin

Saccharin is an artificial sweetener that is used instead of sugar. It is about 300 to 500 times sweeter than sugar.

Who invented saccharin?

Saccharin was invented by a German, Constantin Fahlberg, in the U.S. in 1879.

The saccharin story

Saccharin was invented by accident. In 1879 Ira Remsen, an American chemist, and his German student, Constantin Fahlberg, were investigating chemical reactions. Fahlberg did not wash his hands after working in the laboratory. Later while eating dinner, he noticed sweetness in the bread he was eating. He traced the sweetness back to the chemical by tasting various chemicals in the laboratory. Fahlberg named it saccharin, from the Latin word for sugar, *saccharum*.

Saccharin is an artificial sweetener that is used instead of sugar.

Constantin Fahlberg (1850–1910)

Constantin Fahlberg patented the discovery and went on to become a wealthy man. Ira Remsen became very angry. Remsen once said that "Fahlberg is a scoundrel. It nauseates me to hear my name mentioned in the same breath with him."

How saccharin works

Our tastebuds are sensitive to particular tastes such as sweet, sour, salty, and bitter. Tastebuds are bunches of special nerves called taste receptors. Sugar tastes sweet because sugar molecules react with our sweet taste receptors. Saccharin molecules are the right shape to react with our sweet receptors. Our tastebuds are fooled into thinking that saccharin is sugar.

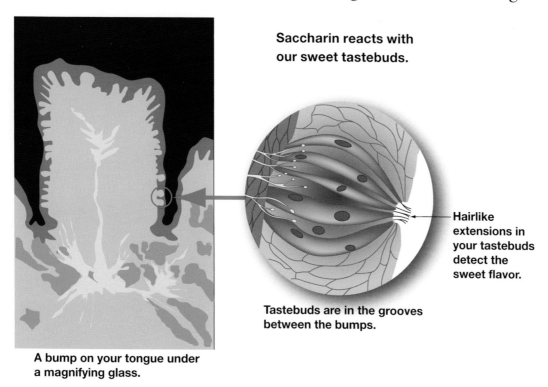

Saccharin reacts with our sweet tastebuds.

Hairlike extensions in your tastebuds detect the sweet flavor.

Tastebuds are in the grooves between the bumps.

A bump on your tongue under a magnifying glass.

Changes to saccharin over time

In 1907, people began to worry about how safe saccharin was and proposed banning it. American President, Theodore Roosevelt, fought the idea. He said, "My doctor gives it to me every day." Since then there have been many scientific studies of saccharin and most people believe it is safe.

Related invention

In 1983, another artificial sweetener called aspartame went on the market in the U.S. Aspartame is about 180 times as sweet as sugar and it is used in diet soft drinks and other diet foods.

Safety pin

A safety pin has a clasp that the sharp end of the pin locks into. This prevents the pin from accidentally jabbing into the person wearing it.

Who invented the safety pin?

Walter Hunt, an American, invented the modern safety pin in 1849.

The safety pin story

Basic types of safety pins have been around for thousands of years. Straight bronze pins were bent with one end being hooked under the other.

Walter Hunt was a mechanic and an inventor. One day he was twisting a piece of wire and came up with the idea for making the safety pin. Hunt's safety pin was different to the previous ones. It was made with one piece of wire which was bent to form a spring and a clasp. He later sold the patent for only $400 because he did not think it was a very good invention.

Safety pins are used to hold things together.

Did you know?

Hunt also invented many other things, including the first sewing machine in the U.S. He did not patent it, because he thought it would cause unemployment.

How safety pins work

The safety pin is made of stiff steel wire. It is bent into a circle at the middle. This makes the ends spring apart when the pin is opened. One end is sharpened to make a point. The other end is fitted with a special rounded guard. When the pin is closed, the springy steel pushes the sharp point into the protective guard, so it stays shut.

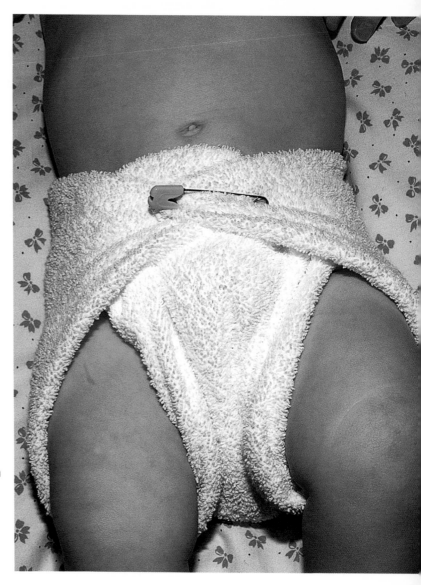

One common use for safety pins is to fasten a baby's diaper.

Changes to safety pins over time

Safety pins now come in all shapes and sizes. They are even used as jewelry and body decorations.

Related inventions

Velcro was invented in Switzerland by Georges de Mestral in 1955. Johan Vaaler, a Norwegian, is credited with inventing the paper clip in 1899.

Scrabble®

Scrabble® is a popular word game. It is played with tiles containing a single letter and a score, on a board that is divided into squares.

Who invented Scrabble®?

Alfred Butts, an American, invented the game which became Scrabble® between 1931 and 1938.

The Scrabble® story

Alfred Butts decided to invent a game when he was unemployed. He called his first attempt Lexico. Games companies were not interested in buying it. He changed the rules of the game and called it Criss-Cross Words.

James Brunot bought the rights to the game from Butts in 1947. He rearranged the squares, made the rules easier, and changed the name to Scrabble®. Brunot and his friends set up a factory and started making sets by hand. It sold poorly at first, but in 1953 they sold over one million sets.

By placing your letters on some squares, you can double or triple your score.

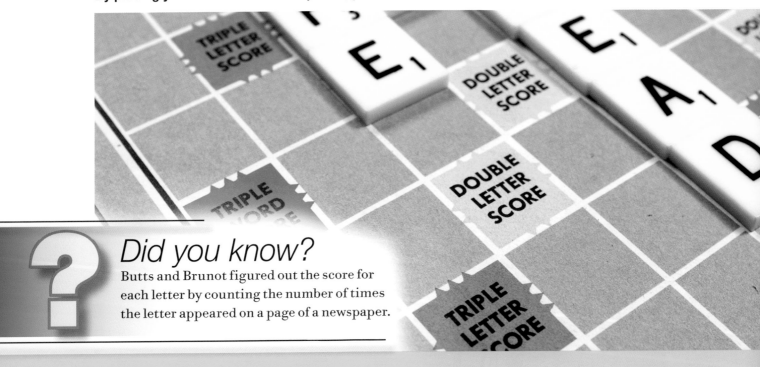

Did you know?

Butts and Brunot figured out the score for each letter by counting the number of times the letter appeared on a page of a newspaper.

How Scrabble® works

In a game of Scrabble®, each player has seven tiles. The tiles have a letter of the alphabet and a score printed on them. The first player puts a word on the board, covering the center square. The players then take turns putting words on the board. The words must use one letter that is already on the board. The words must be in the dictionary and you cannot use proper names.

You gain points after each turn by adding up the value of every letter in your word. Putting your word on certain squares can increase your score.

Scrabble® can be played by up to four players at a time.

Changes to Scrabble® over time

Scrabble® has grown in popularity and it is now the second highest-selling board game behind Monopoly.

Related invention

Parker Brothers released the Monopoly game in 1935. Monopoly was based on the Landlord's Game, which was released in 1904. More than 200 million Monopoly games have been sold worldwide.

Skateboard

A skateboard is a short piece of molded plywood mounted on four wheels. People ride skateboards and perform tricks.

Who invented the skateboard?

No one knows who invented the skateboard. American surf shop owner, Bill Richards, invented the first modern-design skateboard in 1958.

The skateboard story

People in the 1920s and 1930s used to strap rollerskate wheels to planks of wood and ride them down hills. This was very dangerous.

Bill Richards wanted a product that allowed people to imitate surfing on dry land when there were no good waves. He got a rollerskate company to make him special sets of wheels. He bolted these to rectangular pieces of wood and soon people were "sidewalk skating."

Skateboarding is an exciting sport.

Did you know?

Only 100 people came to see the first skateboarding competition in 1964. One year later skateboard championships were televised on American national television.

How skateboards work

The board of a skateboard is called the deck. The wheels are attached to the deck using metal parts called trucks. The wheels have bearings to let them turn freely.

The rider stands on the deck and pushes against the ground to move forwards. You can change direction by putting one foot at the back of the deck to lift up the front wheels.

Skateboarding can be a dangerous sport. Riders must wear safety equipment such as helmets, knee pads, and elbow pads to protect them from injuries when they fall off.

deck

wheels

bearings

trucks

Changes to skateboards over time

Skateboard decks are now made from fiberglass to make them stronger and more flexible. The wheels have the latest bearings so that they roll better and travel more smoothly over rough surfaces.

Related invention

American brothers, Scott and Brennan Olson, found a very old set of rollerskates that had the wheels in a line. The brothers experimented with this design. In 1979, they attached modern wheels to ice hockey boots and invented rollerblades.

Sliced bread

Sliced bread is bread that has been sliced and wrapped before it is delivered to the stores.

Who invented sliced bread?

Otto Rohwedder, an American, invented sliced bread in 1928.

The sliced bread story

Rohwedder came up with the idea of selling sliced bread in 1912, but his first attempts were not very successful. At first he tried to keep the slices together with hatpins.

The main problem was that the bread went stale quickly. He finally overcame this in 1928 by wrapping the sliced bread in waxed paper. Two years later sliced bread was being sold across the U.S.

The process of slicing and packaging bread is now automated.

Did you know?

The sandwich is named after English gambler John Montague, the Earl of Sandwich. He was once involved in a game of cards that went on for over 24 hours. He asked for meat and slices of bread to be brought to him so he could eat without having to leave the game.

How sliced bread works

Flour, sugar, **yeast**, and water are mixed together to make dough. The yeast feeds on the sugar and makes gas. The flour has an elastic substance called gluten. It catches the gas, forming bubbles in the dough. The dough rises as the bubbles get bigger. Baking the dough kills the yeast and makes bread.

The loaves of bread are then sliced and put into plastic bags to prevent them from going stale.

This is an advertisement for sliced bread from the 1960s.

Hey! That's the last Sunblest sandwich

With Sunblest bread, sandwiches suddenly become an exciting meal. That wonderful just-baked flavour gives your appetite a lift, makes you wish you'd made twice as many of these delicious Sunblest sandwiches.

Sunblest bread — white or brown — is the finest there is, baked by only the best bakers. That is why Sunblest is always fresh, tasty and full of nourishment. It's the reason that wise mothers everywhere insist on bread with the Sunblest symbol. They know they can give their families no better.

GIVE YOUR FAMILY AN EXTRA TREAT. TAKE HOME ONE OF THESE SPECIAL SUNBLEST LOAVES TODAY

Sunblest bread is good bread
FRESH TO THE LAST SLICE
MADE ONLY BY MEMBERS OF THE QUALITY BAKERS OF BRITAIN

Changes to sliced bread over time

Sliced bread now comes in plastic bags. The bags are closed with plastic tags that have the date the bread was made printed on them.

Related invention

U.S. company General Electric invented the electric toaster in 1913. The first sliced bread was rather thick for sandwiches, but it was just right for toast. It led to an increase in the popularity of the electric toaster.

Soft drink

Soft drink is any sweet fizzy drink that does not contain alcohol.

Who invented soft drink?

In 1768, an Englishman called Joseph Priestly made the first fizzy, or soda, water.

The soft drink story

Mineral water from natural springs in the ground is sometimes fizzy. People have known for hundreds of years that this water is good for you. In the 1700s, people experimented with ways of making fizzy water like the natural mineral water. Joseph Priestly was the first person to do this successfully. People then began to add flavors and herbs to the mineral water. They added things such as sarsaparilla, sugar, and fruit. Some historians believe that the first flavored soft drink was made in 1807 by Dr. Philip Syng Physick in the U.S.

Bubbles of carbon dioxide gas make soft drink fizzy.

Joseph Priestly (1733–1804)

Joseph Priestly was a minister of religion who had never studied science. In 1766 he met the famous inventor Benjamin Franklin, who inspired him to experiment with electricity and chemistry. As well as inventing soda water, Joseph Priestly discovered oxygen, hydrochloric acid, and laughing gas.

How soft drinks work

Soft drinks are made from water and sugar, with colors and flavors added. The fizz comes from carbon dioxide gas which is pumped in under pressure and dissolves in the soft drink. When you take the lid off, there is a hissing noise as the gas "undissolves" and makes bubbles in the drink. If the lid is loose, the gas escapes and the soft drink goes flat.

Metal soft drink bottle caps needed a special opener.

Changes to soft drinks over time

Many soft drinks contain a large amount of sugar, so more and more soft drinks now use artificial sweeteners. Naturally flavored mineral water is becoming more popular because it contains less sugar.

Related invention

In 1892 the "Crown Cork Bottle Seal" was patented by William Painter in the U.S. It was a metal cap that required a special opener to remove it. This was the first successful way of keeping bubbles in a glass soft drink bottle.

A stapler is a common tool found in offices and homes. It is used to join pieces of paper using thin strips of metal called staples.

Who invented the stapler?

The stapler was invented by an Englishman, Charles Henry Gould, in 1868.

The stapler story

During the early 1800s, sheets of paper were held together in all sorts of ways. Some had holes poked in them and were tied together with string, ribbon, or tape. Others were pinned or glued together.

Gould invented the first stapler in 1868. It was a big machine and he used it for bookbinding.

The first desktop stapler was patented in 1877. It worked by pushing metallic staples through the pages and bending them closed. It only held one staple at a time.

An early stapler

Stapler timeline

1868	1877	1878	1927
Gould invented the stapler	The first desktop stapler was invented	The first stapler to hold many staples was invented	Staples were glued together in rows so they were easier to insert

How staplers work

A stapler has two arms hinged together at one end. There is a guide tray and a blade in the top arm and a groove on the bottom arm.

A row of glued-together staples is put into the guide tray. It is pushed forward by a spring. The front staple rests over an opening.

Pushing down on the top of the stapler makes the blade push the front staple down through the opening and the sheets of paper. The ends of the staple are pushed into the groove on the bottom arm of the stapler. This curves the ends of the staple and holds the paper together.

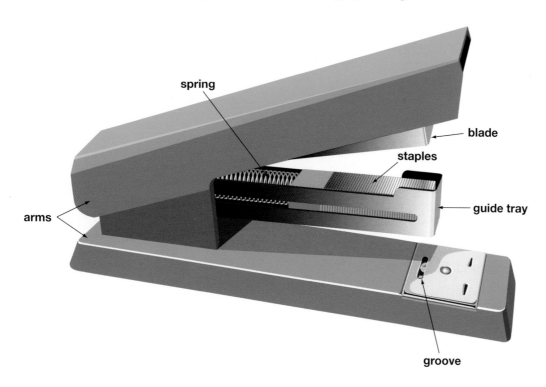

Changes to staplers over time

Special staplers are now used in surgery to reduce the size of peoples' stomachs so they cannot eat as much food as they used to.

Related invention

Johan Vaaler, a Norwegian, is credited with inventing the paper clip in 1899.

Sunscreen

Sunscreen is a lotion or cream that is put on your skin to help protect it from the harmful rays of the sun.

Who invented sunscreen?

The first sunscreen was invented by Eugene Schueller, in France in 1936.

The sunscreen story

In the early 1930s, South Australian chemist Milton Blake experimented to produce a sunburn cream, but he was not successful. Eugene Schueller was the founder of the L'Oreal cosmetic company, where sunscreen was first invented. In the early 1940s, Dr. Benjamin Green, a physician from Miami, developed a sunscreen to protect soldiers fighting in World War II. He then began experimenting with different formulas and discovered the recipe for Coppertone suntan cream in 1944.

Zinc cream was invented in 1940.

$\mathcal{S}$unscreen timeline

Around 500 BCE	1936	1940	1980
Ancient Greeks used olive oil as a type of sunscreen	The first sunscreen was invented in France	An Australian company invented zinc cream	The first UVA/UVB sunscreen was invented

How sunscreen works

Sunscreens block two types of harmful ultraviolet, or UV, rays from the sun. These rays are UVA rays, which give you a suntan and UVB rays, which cause sunburn, wrinkles, and skin cancer. Sunscreens contain different chemicals to absorb both kinds of rays. Sunscreens are labelled with a Sun Protection Factor, or SPF, that says how much protection they give. If you can normally go out in the sun for 10 minutes without burning and you apply an SPF10 sunscreen, then you would not burn for 100 minutes (10 x 10 = 100).

This sunscreen has an SPF of 15.

Changes to sunscreen over time

Doctors are now advising people to cover up and stay out of the sun, especially in the middle of the day. Many people now choose spray-on tans instead of a real suntan.

Related invention
The first sunglasses were invented in the 1700s.

Index

Page references in bold indicate that there is a full entry for that invention.